THE KIDS' LIBRARY OF MARTIAL ARTS™

AIKIDO

Pamela Randall

The Rosen Publishing Group's
PowerKids Press™
New York

Published in 1999 by The Rosen Publishing Group, Inc.
29 East 21st Street, New York, NY 10010

First Edition

Book Design: Danielle Primiceri

Photo Illustrations by Seth Dinnerman

Randall, Pamela.
    Aikido / by Pamela Randall.
        p.   cm. — (The kids' library of martial arts)
    Includes index.
    Summary: Introduces the history, basic moves, and terminology of this martial art.
    ISBN 0-8239-5234-7
    1. Aikido—Juvenile literature. [1. Aikido.] I. Title. II. Series: Randall, Pamela. The kids' library of martial arts.
    GV1114.35.R36 1998
    796.815'4—dc21

                                       97-49274
                                            CIP
                                            AC

Manufactured in the United States of America

Contents

生力心身

357548

Paul and Amy Go to the Dojo

Paul and Amy are new students at the aikido **dojo** (DOH-joh). Aikido is a **martial art** (MAR-shul ART) that is a little bit like karate. A dojo is a school where aikido is taught and practiced. In the dojo, there are mats on the floor and a **shrine** (SHRYN) at one end of the room. The shrine is in memory of Morehei Ueshiba, the person who created aikido. He was better known as **O Sensei** (OH SEN-say), or "great teacher." O Sensei lived from 1883 to 1969. In honor of him, each aikido teacher is called sensei.

◀ *Stretching before you practice aikido or any martial art is important.*

The Creation of Aikido

O Sensei had studied many other martial arts when he was young. He also studied sword fighting, **spear** (SPEER) fighting, and **sumo** (SOO-moh) wrestling. But O Sensei wanted people to learn how to settle **conflicts** (KON-flikts) in a peaceful way. That is why he named his martial art aikido. Aikido means "the way of harmony" in Japanese.

O Sensei worked out the basic moves and beliefs of aikido and opened his first studio in Japan, where he lived. The first dojo outside of Japan opened in Hawaii in 1961.

Aikido was created in Japan, which is part of East Asia. All martial arts came from East Asia. ▶

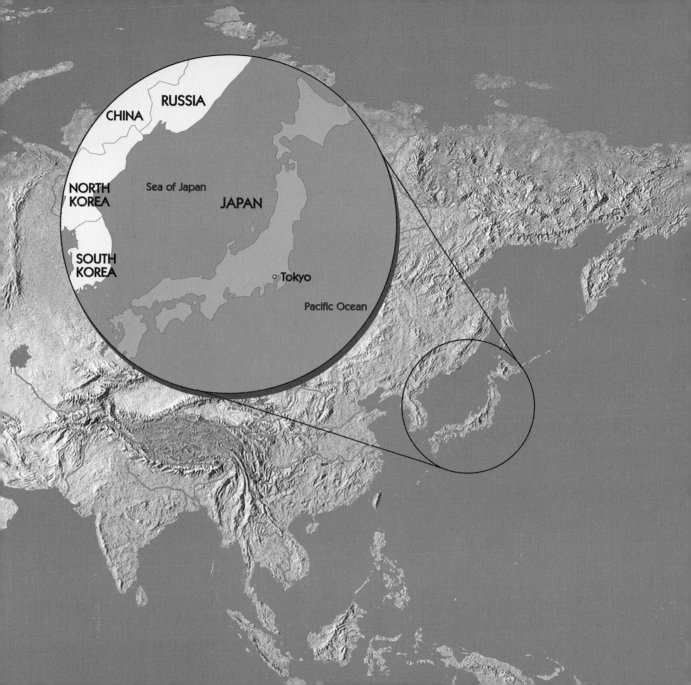

More Aikido Facts

O Sensei wanted to train people's minds and spirits as well as their bodies. He never wanted people to use aikido for fighting. Instead, aikido is used only to end fights peacefully.

If an **aggressor** (uh-GRESS-er) does start a fight, the use of aikido can end it quickly. And no one will get hurt. You see, the **defender** (de-FEN-dur), called *nagi* (NAH-gee), can use aikido to protect himself without hurting the aggressor.

◄ *Students of aikido should always listen carefully to the lessons their sensei teaches them.*

The Center of Energy

Aikido teaches that it's important to focus and direct your **vital** (VY-tuhl) life energy. The word for this energy is *ki* (KEE). The middle part of the name "aikido" comes from this word.

Aikido also teaches that the center of your *ki* is in your pelvis, which is just below your belly button. Your energy flows from your pelvis out to your arms and legs. This is why all movements in aikido begin in the pelvis. The motions of aikido are usually flowing and **circular** (SIR-kyoo-ler).

Aikido teaches students to direct their energy in the proper way. ▶

Aikido's Ranking System

In aikido, as in other martial arts, students are **promoted** (proh-MOH-ted) as they get better from one level to the next. These levels are called ranks.

In most martial arts, teachers decide when to advance students by watching them **compete** (kum-PEET) with each other. But in aikido, promotion from one rank to the next is not based on competition. Instead, promotions are based on testing each student individually.

◀ *The sensei watches his student carefully to see if he has learned all his moves correctly.*

Getting Started

Amy and Paul will start their aikido classes in the lowest rank. The lower ranks are all called **kyus** (KYOOZ). As they learn aikido, both Paul and Amy will be promoted from one *kyu* to another.

Paul will practice being the defender. Amy will pretend to be the aggressor. Then they will switch roles so that they are both able to practice all the moves.

As they practice and learn more about aikido, Paul and Amy will advance to the higher ranks. These are called **dans** (DAHNZ).

Many moves in aikido involve throwing an opponent off balance to defeat her. ▶

Black and White Belts

When Paul and Amy take their first aikido class, they will each wear a heavy white cotton suit called a *gi* (GEE). This suit has a jacket and pants along with a belt.

In many aikido schools, or clubs, all students in the lower ranks wear white belts. In others, students get different colored belts as they advance through the ranks. Students in the higher ranks wear black belts.

The rules are often different from one school to another. Usually, there are five *kyus* and up to ten *dans* that students can go through as they advance.

The color of your belt lets people know how much you are learning.

Shiho-Nige

One of the most important things that Amy and Paul will learn in aikido class is *shiho-nige* (SHEE-hoh-NEE-gay). *Shiho-nige* is a way of throwing an **opponent** (uh-POH-nent). Paul will learn how to step out and turn while taking the opponent's wrist.

Then he will lift that person's wrist and turn again. By swinging down, he will be able to throw the opponent down! The circular movement Paul uses will help him keep his balance. And neither Paul nor his opponent gets hurt!

A Matter of Balance

Aikido teaches the importance of balance. A person practicing aikido learns to keep his balance even when it's difficult to do so. At the same time, he practices throwing his opponent off-balance.

An aikido student learns to decide quickly what moves her opponent will use on her. Soon, Amy will be able to tell if her opponent is going to grab her, kick her, or punch her. There are aikido moves to defend yourself against every kind of move. Amy will also have to decide quickly what moves she will use against her opponent.

◀ *Aikido students are taught how to fall down without hurting themselves.*

Many Forms of Aikido

O Sensei developed aikido using certain moves. Over time, other teachers of aikido have slightly changed some of O Sensei's moves. Others have created new moves. But the basic beliefs of aikido don't change.

One thing that *will* change is the color of Amy's and Paul's belts. They both hope to earn black belts one day.

Glossary

aggressor (uh-GRESS-er) A person who starts a fight.

circular (SIR-kyoo-ler) Something that has the shape of a circle.

compete (kum-PEET) Trying hard to win something.

conflict (KON-flikt) A fight or a struggle.

dans (DAHNZ) The higher ranks in aikido.

defender (de-FEN-dur) A person protecting himself in a fight.

dojo (DOH-joh) A school where aikido is practiced.

gi (GEE) A heavy cotton suit worn when practicing aikido.

ki (KEE) A Japanese word meaning vital life energy.

kyus (KYOOZ) The lower ranks in aikido.

martial art (MAR-shul ART) Any of the arts of self-defense that are practiced as a sport.

nagi (NAH-gee) A Japanese word meaning defender.

opponent (uh-POH-nent) A person who is on the other side in a fight or a game.

O Sensei (OH SEN-say) The man who created aikido.

promoted (proh-MOH-ted) To be raised in rank or importance.

shiho-nige (SHEE-hoh-NEE-gay) A Japanese term for the way to throw someone using aikido.

shrine (SHRYN) A special place built in honor of a holy or important person.

spear (SPEER) A long wooden stick with a sharp point.

sumo (SOO-moh) A Japanese form of wrestling.

vital (VY-tuhl) Something that is very important.

Index